SHE'S A MOMMA, NOT A MOVIE STAR

A ROSE IS ROSE Collection by Pat Brady

Andrews and McMeel
A Universal Press Syndicate Company
Kansas City

Read *Rose Is Rose* in your local newspaper
and on the World Wide Web:
http://www.unitedmedia.com/comics/roseisrose/

Send Pat Brady e-mail at: pbrady8222@AOL.COM

Send Pat Brady paper mail at:
Pat Brady (*Rose Is Rose*)
United Media
200 Madison Ave.
New York, NY 10016

FAX Pat Brady at (815) 895-0302

THERE ARE BILLIONS OF STARS IN THE SKY...

GALAXIES OF EVERY DESCRIPTION, SWIRLING ENDLESSLY IN INFINITE PATTERNS ABOVE US!

I SUPPOSE, WITH THE NUMBER OF BABIES MOTHER NATURE PUTS TO BED EVERY NIGHT...

SHE NEEDED TO HANG A HECK OF A MOBILE!

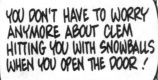

WHAT A SPECTACULAR SUNSET!

MOVE, PASQUALE, SO YOUR **SHADOW** CAN SEE IT TOO!

OTHER WAY! HE'S TRYING TO LOOK AROUND YOU!

HURRY! THE SUNSET'S ALMOST OVER!

WHERE'D HE GO?

HE'S HARD TO FIND AT NIGHT! WE'LL NEED A FLASHLIGHT!

THERE HE IS! HE FINALLY GOT AROUND YOU, BUT TOO LATE!

SORRY.

14

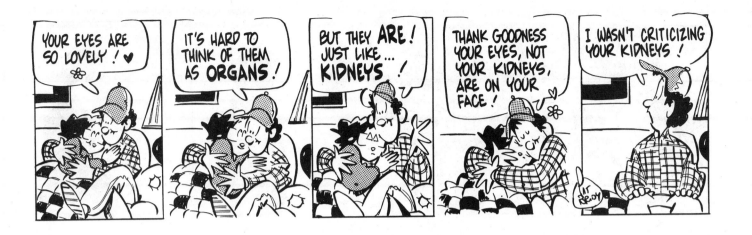

FIRST, SET YOUR SIGHTS ON WHAT YOU **WANT** IN LIFE, MIMI...

THEN, WHEN YOUR GOAL COMES WITHIN REACH, **GO** FOR IT WITHOUT HESITATION!

:GRAB:

WIGGLE WIGGLE

WHY DO YOU HUG FOR SO **LONG**?

BECAUSE I NEVER KNOW WHICH HUG WILL BE MY LAST.

MY EYES ARE EMPTY.

WE'LL REFILL THEM IN THE MORNING.

16

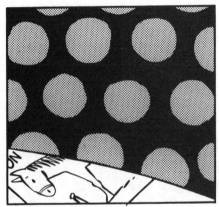

28

ARE YOU GOING TO SAY "NYAH-NA-NYAH" AND MAKE FUN OF ME FOR FALLING?

OF COURSE NOT! I'VE FALLEN MANY TIMES!

YOU HAVE?!

YES, I HAVE!

NYAH-NA NYAH!!

"EVEN A FOOL, WHEN HE HOLDETH HIS PEACE, IS COUNTED WISE..."

"AND HE THAT SHUTTETH HIS LIPS IS ESTEEMED A MAN OF UNDERSTANDING."

KING SOLOMON SAID THAT.

NOT JUST BECAUSE HE WANTED TO WATCH TV INSTEAD OF TALK!

34

: SNIFF :
: SNIFF :
MMM !

WE BAKED BROWNIES TODAY ! PASQUALE'S BEEN SAVING THE AROMA FOR YOU !

PAT BRADY

YOU'RE RIGHT! I COULD'VE TAKEN PASQUALE TO THE PLAYGROUND OR THE MUSEUM THIS AFTERNOON...

INSTEAD OF TREATING MYSELF TO A BUBBLE BATH WHILE HE WATCHED TV! OKAY, OKAY!

WHO ARE YOU TALKING TO?

I CALL THEM THE "LOUSY-MOM GOBLINS"!

YOU SAY YOU'RE SOMETIMES HARASSED BY "LOUSY-MOM GOBLINS"?

YES! THEY LIKE TO POINT OUT WAYS IN WHICH I FAIL TO BE A PERFECT MOTHER!

GOOD HEAVENS, ROSE!

YOU THINK I'M CRAZY, RIGHT?

NO, I'M WONDERING WHETHER THEY KNOW THE "CRUMMY-DAD GNOMES"!

HEY, PASQUALE, WHAT WOULD HAPPEN IF I POINTED THE REMOTE CONTROL AT MYSELF AND PRESSED "REWIND"?

:PRESS:

"REWIND" PRESSED AND MYSELF AT CONTROL REMOTE THE POINTED I IF HAPPEN WOULD WHAT, PASQUALE, HEY?

MOMMM!!!

IT'S IMPORTANT TO GIVE HIM THE HOME COURT ADVANTAGE IN HIS GAME OF LIFE.

:MUNCH: :MUNCH:

>MUNCH: >MUNCH:

WHAT SHOULD I DO WITH THE PEACH'S BRAIN?

THESE ARE YOUR FOOTPRINTS, MADE IN THE HOSPITAL THE DAY YOU WERE BORN!

IT MUST'VE BEEN A REALLY DIRTY HOSPITAL!

DING ♪

QUIET IN THE ELEVATOR, WASN'T IT?

IT'S LIKE A TINY CHURCH FILLED WITH LIBRARIANS!

A PHONE CALL TO HER PARENTS HAS RETURNED ROSE TO CHILDHOOD

A PHONE CALL TO HER PARENTS HAS RETURNED ROSE TO CHILDHOOD

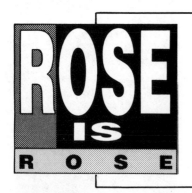

47

The thrill seeker risks a tickle, and lives to tell about it.

56

THE HOUSEWORK'S DONE, SUPPER'S ON THE STOVE...

I'LL OPEN UP THE KITCHEN AND LET IN SOME FRESH AIR!

WOOO! THERE'S THE EARRING I LOST!

SOME DAYS EVERYTHING JUST RUNS SMOOTHLY, THAT'S ALL!

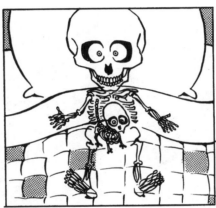

WHEN OTHERS HAVE MORE THAN YOU, DON'T CRY... COUNT YOUR BLESSINGS INSTEAD!

WATCH, I'LL COUNT MINE, TO SHOW YOU HOW!

LET'S SEE... I CAN **FLY**... I CAN BE **INVISIBLE** WHENEVER I WANT... I NEVER HAVE TO GO TO BED ... IT'S ALWAYS MY **BIRTHDAY**...

OKAY, OKAY, MAYBE MY BLESSINGS ARE COOLER THAN YOURS...

I DON'T NEED SLEEP! FOR ME, THERE'S NO SUCH THING AS TIME!

FOR ME, A DAY IS LIKE A THOUSAND YEARS, AND A THOUSAND YEARS IS LIKE A DAY!

YOU CAN'T USE THE SAME EXCUSES *I* DO!

LEAH, I'D LIKE YOU TO LOOK OVER THIS BABY SITTER JOB APPLICATION FORM AND...

UM...

FOLD FOLD FOLD FOLD
FOLD FOLD FOLD FOLD
FOLD FOLD FOLD FOLD
FOLD   FOLD
FOLD   FOLD
FOLD   FOLD
FOLD
FOLD

WELL, YES, ORIGAMI SKILLS ARE A PLUS!

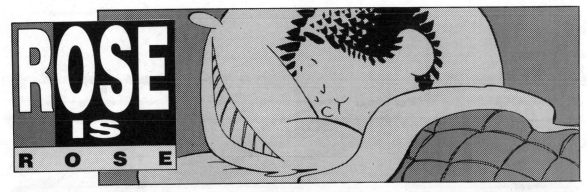

63

64

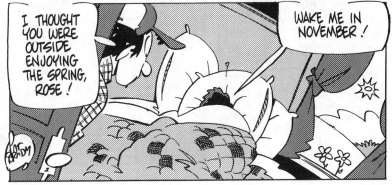

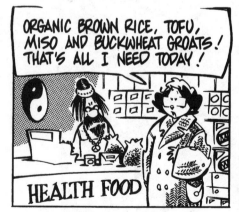

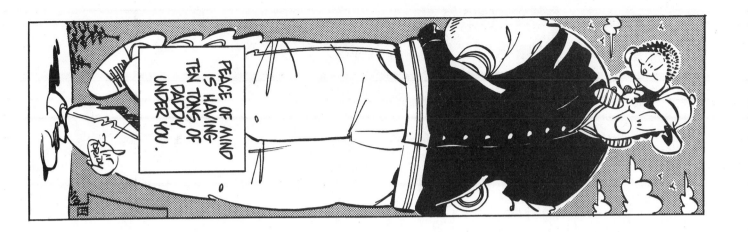

IT'S THE SOLUTION TO MY MENTAL BLOCK ABOUT USING PUBLIC RESTROOMS, ROSE!

A **VIRTUAL REALITY** SYSTEM, PROGRAMMED TO MAKE IT SEEM EXACTLY...

...LIKE I'M **HOME**, IN MY **OWN** BATHROOM!

HOW'S IT WORKING, JIMBO?

HEY! WATCH IT, BUDDY!!

MEN

KNOCK KNOCK

:GASP: WHAT TIME IS IT?! OH, MY GOODNESS!

WE'RE AT THE HOME OF **ROSE GUMBO**, KNOWN AS "THE NO LUNCH MOM"...

POLICE

NEWS NEWS

"THE SIX O'CLOCK NEWS CAMERA CREW": DREADFUL IMAGE #259 IN THE MIND OF AN IMPERFECT MOM

SORRY THIS IS LATE!

THE PENCIL SHARPENER WON'T DO ANYTHING!

IT'S PROBABLY **FULL!**

WHEN DO YOU THINK IT WILL BE HUNGRY AGAIN?

GOODNESS, NO, WE'RE NOT ALWAYS **SERIOUS** IN HEAVEN!

THE FACT THAT RAINDROPS ARE SHAPED LIKE LITTLE WATER BALLOONS SHOULD GIVE YOU A CLUE!

BEFORE PUTTING ON CLOTHES FROM A DRYER...

IT'S BETTER TO WAIT UNTIL THE STATIC ELECTRICITY DIES DOWN!

ESPECIALLY PEOPLE WITH ONLY TWO HAIRS!

MMM! NICE, BUT...

OOO! VERY NICE, BUT...

OH, YES, YES, **NOW** WE'RE THERE!

NICE TREE, PASQUALE! IT LOOKS AS REAL AS MOTHER NATURE'S!

DID SHE PLAY WITH CLAY WHEN SHE WAS YOUNG?

OH, SHE'S FOREVER YOUNG!

I'M SORRY I'VE BEEN IN SUCH A NASTY MOOD...

I DON'T KNOW WHY YOU PUT UP WITH ME!

A SAILOR RIDES OUT THE STORM WITHOUT LOSING HIS LOVE FOR THE SEA.

WELL, YOU'RE IN A GOOD MOOD! WHAT HAVE YOU BEEN DOING?

SAILING!

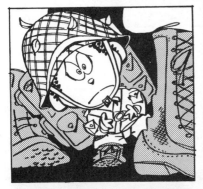

STEPPING ONTO AN ESCALATOR GETS EASIER WITH PRACTICE.!

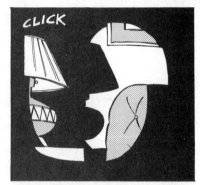

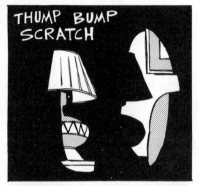

SUNRISE

SUNSET

MY SHADOW **STRETCHES** WHEN HE WAKES UP IN THE MORNING AND BEFORE HE GOES TO SLEEP AT NIGHT!

DOESN'T EVERYONE?

WHO'S BEEN FOOLING WITH THE ADJUSTMENT DIAL ON THE SCALE?

WHAT'S THE HARDEST THING IN THE WORLD TO DO?

TO GO EASY ON YOURSELF!

THAT'S A GOOD **MOM** ANSWER!

YOU HAVE NO IDEA!

Your eyelashes are as soft and quiet as falling stars, and just as thrilling.

THE REMOTE CONTROL IS WORKING ON PEEKABOO TOO!

OOOOH!

TOES AND MUD WERE MADE FOR EACH OTHER!

FRANKLY I CONSIDER THEM TWO OF MY BEST IDEAS!

PASQUALE, WHAT ARE YOU DOING UP SO LATE?

YOU HAVEN'T LAUGHED YET!

I CAN NEVER GO TO SLEEP UNTIL I HEAR YOU AND DADDY LAUGHING IN THE KITCHEN!

REALLY? THAT'S SO CUTE... HA HA HA...

HO HO HO

Z

YOU NEVER APPRECIATE ANYTHING I DO!

I SUPPOSE YOU'RE RIGHT, ROSE... THE TRUTH IS I LOVE YOU FOR YOUR LOOKS ALONE.

WHOA!

YOUR EYES LOOK REALLY PRETTY TONIGHT!

I GAINED ONE POUND SINCE YESTERDAY!

THE LONGEST JOURNEY BEGINS WITH A SINGLE STEP, MY LOVE!

MOST WOMEN PREFER NOT TO JOURNEY IN THE DIRECTION YOU LIKE!

AT A POUND A DAY, YOU COULD BE OVER 300 BY CHRISTMAS!

PURRRRRRR

I KNEW SOONER OR LATER YOU'D LIE DOWN ON THE WHOLE WORLD!

MY WORDS TRAVEL AT OVER SEVEN HUNDRED MILES AN HOUR!

THEN DON'T BLAME ME WHEN THEY GO IN ONE EAR AND OUT THE OTHER!

OH, DEAR!

AH! I WAS AFRAID I HAD FORGOTTEN YOUR SUNBLOCK!

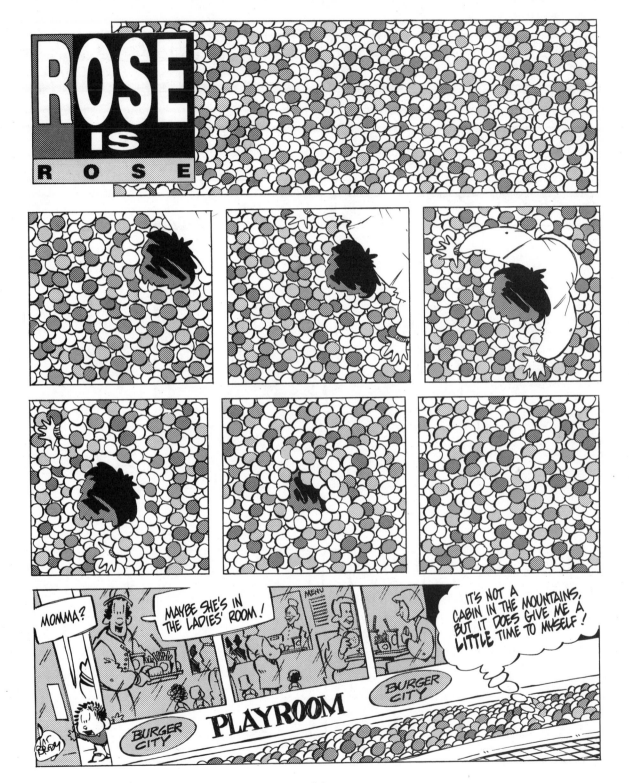

THAT'S ENOUGH TV, PASQUALE! TRY **READING**, LIKE **I** DO!

YOU DON'T HAVE TO READ **WHERE** I DO!

IF I **SLEPT** AS MUCH AS YOU, I'D **STRETCH** AS MUCH AS YOU!

I KNOW YOU PRIDE YOURSELF ON BEING A TERROR, CLEM...

BUT ONCE IN A WHILE, YOU STILL GIVE ME A WARM FUZZY FEELING!

I... I SOMETIMES GIVE WARM FUZZIES?

DON'T BEAT YOURSELF UP ABOUT IT! IT'S NEVER ON PURPOSE!

CLEM, DID I HURT YOUR SELF-IMAGE BY SAYING YOU GIVE ME WARM FUZZY FEELINGS?

I'M SORRY! I SHOULD SPEAK MORE CAUTIOUSLY AROUND SUCH A...

SENSITIVE GUY.

AAAAAAA

I GET PROTECTIVE FEELINGS WHEN A STRANGER NEARS PASQUALE!

GOBBLE MUNCH CHEW GULP SCARF WOLF GNAW CRUNCH BOLT EAT

POPCORN

POPCORN

YOU OFFER ME THE UNPOPPED ONE?!

POPCORN

NO, I WANT YOU TO POP IT FOR ME!

POPCORN

LOOK, PASQUALE, IT'S YOUR **TEACHER**! HI, MS. HARRIS!

PASQUALE IS SURPRISED TO SEE YOU IN A SUPERMARKET!

HE DOESN'T QUITE KNOW WHAT TO DO!

DOES ANYBODY KNOW WHERE THE CEREAL AISLE IS?

IT WAS A BAD DREAM, PASQUALE! I'M HERE NOW! GO BACK TO SLEEP!

:Z:

AFTER A NIGHTMARE, A GUY LIKE ME LOOKS TOO SPOOKY!

I CAN'T TICKLE MYSELF!

NOBODY CAN!

I'VE NEVER BEEN TICKLED AT ALL!

NEVER?

WHEN YOU'RE "ONE WITH EVERYTHING" IT'S IMPOSSIBLE!

ROOT B...

FROM A BEE'S POINT OF VIEW I SUPPOSE A ROOT BEER IS A FAIR TRADE FOR HONEY!

96

:PSST: JIMBO! IT IS I, **THE AMAZING PERPLEXKIN**, THE MIND READER!

YOU'RE ABOUT TO HAVE A CONVERSATION WITH YOUR WIFE! YOU'LL BE NEEDING ME!

DO YOU STILL WANT TO DROP PASQUALE AT HIS GRANDMOTHER'S TONIGHT, AND SPEND A ROMANTIC EVENING TOGETHER?

SURE! WHY?

I THINK I HAVE THE **FLU**!

YOUR FIRST IMPULSE IS TO SAY SOMETHING **CONSIDERATE**, LIKE "WE'LL POSTPONE OUR PLANS UNTIL YOU'RE FEELING BETTER, HONEY!" RIGHT?

RIGHT!

WELL, FORGET IT! SHE WANTS YOU TO **INSIST** ON FOLLOWING THROUGH WITH THE ROMANTIC EVENING! SHE WANTS YOU TO BE WILLING TO RISK CATCHING THE FLU, JUST TO BE NEAR HER!

ROSE, WE'RE **NOT** CHANGING PLANS! **I DON'T CARE** IF YOU'RE SICK!

:SQUEAL:

GOSH, THANKS, AMAZING PERPLEXKIN!

MUST RUN! TWO BILLION MORE STOPS TO MAKE!

97

I'M HOME. GREAT!

WELCOME HOME, JIMBO, YOU WONDERFUL GUY, YOU! IT'S SO NICE TO SEE YOU, YOU'RE SO SPECIAL TO ME!

OH, ROSE, YOU'RE A SIGHT FOR SORE EYES! I MISSED YOU SO MUCH TODAY! HERE, LET ME HELP YOU WITH THAT!

I MUST LOVE YOU, JIMBO, IF I PUT UP WITH THIS NONSENSE!

COME HERE, ROSE.

AS LONG AS WE GET HERE, I DON'T CARE WHAT ROUTE WE TAKE!

100

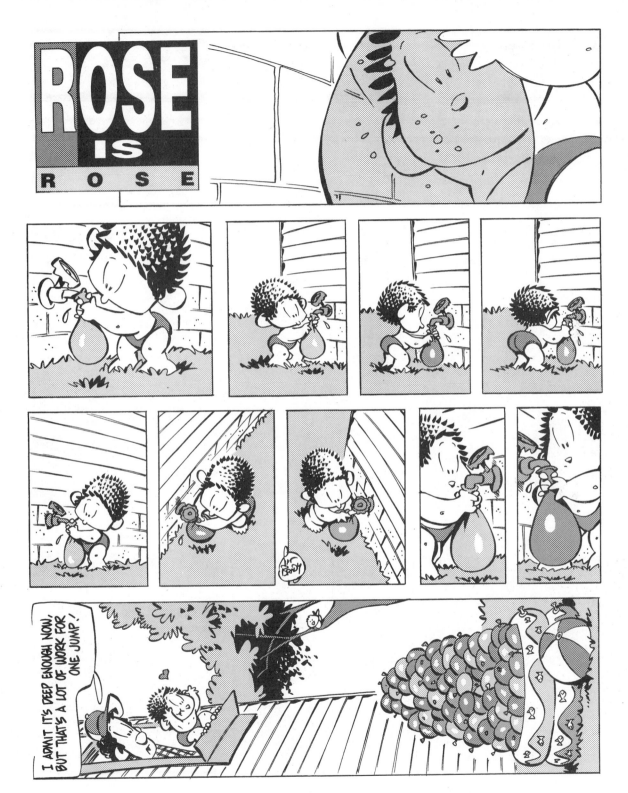

IT'S SAFETY-MINDED TO CARRY A FLASHLIGHT AT NIGHT!

YES, BECAUSE IF WE SEE A MONSTER WE CAN SCARE HIM AWAY LIKE THIS!

:LICK:

:RUB:

:LICK:

FLIP

MIMI, I LICK MY FINGERS TO **TURN THE PAGES** OF MY COOKBOOK!

I KANT TAYST **ANY** OF DEEZ RESSAPEEZ!

WHEN I WAS A BOY MY FAVORITE SPOT WAS MY PEEPAW'S TOOLSHED WHERE HE KEPT HIS HUBCAP COLLECTION...

THE COOLEST WAS A CUSTOM "FULL MOON" THAT PEEPAW GOT AFTER A '55 DESOTO HIT A POTHOLE!

I WISH YOU COULD'VE SEEN IT, ROSE!

ONCE IN A WHILE ROMANCE AND GUY THINGS CROSS PATHS!

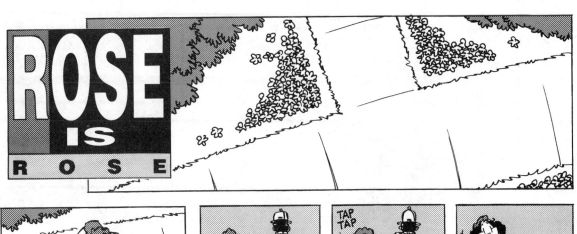

HERE COME THE LIGHTNING BUGS, PASQUALE!

THAT MEANS THE THUNDER BUGS AND RAIN BUGS CAN'T BE FAR AWAY!

WHEN I LISTEN REALLY, **REALLY** HARD, I CAN HEAR THE THUNDER BUGS, I THINK!

SQUIRT

...AND IT TICKLES WHEN THE RAIN BUGS BITE! **HURRY**!

THESE SOUND LIKE **DADDY'S** KIND OF CRITTERS!

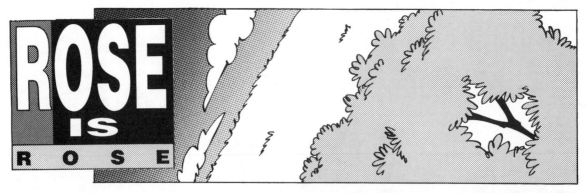

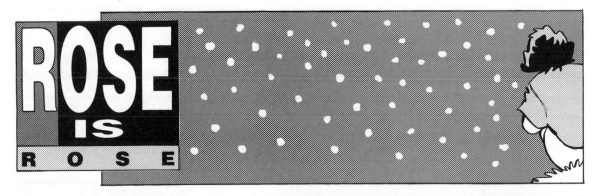

I'M HOME! WHAT'S FOR DINNER?

KISSES! HOW DO YOU LIKE YOURS?

WELL DONE!

THE MANAGEMENT CANNOT BE HELD RESPONSIBLE FOR KISSES ORDERED WELL DONE!

I'VE ALWAYS THOUGHT THE MANAGEMENT WAS A LITTLE TOO RESPONSIBLE ANYWAY!

WHAT'S THIS FOR DESSERT?

SPAGHETTI!

I JUST WANT DESSERT!

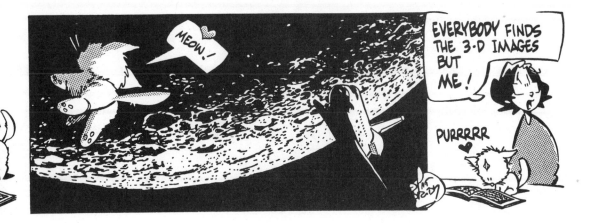

115

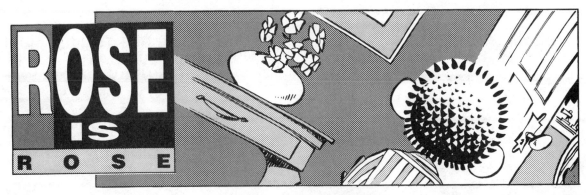

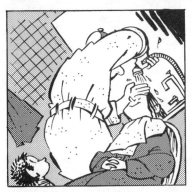

HAVEN'T YOU LEARNED HOW TO WASH YOUR OWN HAIR YET?

WE'VE LEARNED A LOT OF THINGS.

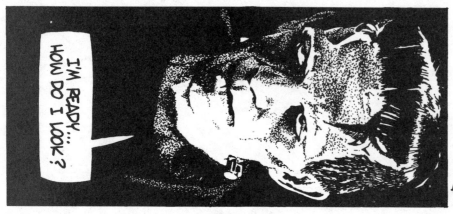

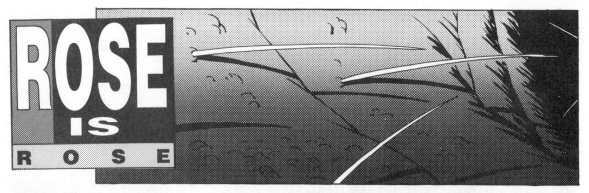

ONE ELEMENT OF SUCCESS IS BEING IN THE RIGHT PLACE AT THE RIGHT TIME!

WHAT IF YOU CAN'T TELL TIME OR READ MAPS?

ANOTHER ELEMENT IS LUCK...

WHEN WE WERE KIDS, GROWNUPS WOULD GIVE US NASTY LOOKS FOR ACTING SILLY IN PUBLIC. :GIGGLE:

MUNCH MUNCH MUNCH

DO WE EMBARRASS YOU IN PUBLIC, PASQUALE?

I JUST WANT YOU TO BE LIKE OTHER MOMMAS AND DADDIES!

WHAT DOES THAT MEAN?

IT MEANS YOU SHOULD BE FAT AND HE SHOULD WEAR BOW TIES

I AGREE WITH THE YOU-FAT PART!